1

CHAPTER 1

Hanging around the clock tower.

I WAS born in Merthyr Tydfil in June 1944.

Six weeks after I was born my father Bryn Edwards was killed when he was struck by a train while working for the Ministry of Defence in a tunnel which was near Caerphilly.

This is the only picture I have got of my father. When I was five years old my mother decided to move to Pricetown, Nantymoel to become a housekeeper for my uncles Emrys, Glyndwr and Evan Edwards who lived in Cadwgan Street.

I hated Nantymoel.

I wanted to go back to Merthyr, and I did run away once but I only got to Danny the Farms before a policeman caught hold of me and took me back home.

My uncle Evan had retired, and my Uncle Glyndwr worked in the Penllwyngwent mine.

The Penllwyngwent was a drift mine working steam coal.

It was opened by the Cory Brothers in 1906 and employed 558 men just prior to Nationalisation in 1947. During 1942 the colliery came under the control of the Powell Duffryn Colliery Company.

The colliery suffered a fire in 1969 and officially closed by the National Coal board on February 7, 1969.

Meanwhile my uncle Emrys taught piano playing lessons in the front room of our home in Cadwgan Street.

And so, I attended Nantymoel Junior School where the headmaster was Mr Fisher.

While I also have memories of a teacher called Miss James.

I did my playing in the bottom yard before stepping up to the top yard.

3

After running home from junior school and being made to listen to "Mrs Dale's Diary" on the radio I would don my daps and leg it down to the Workmen's Hall.I used to sit in the front row chewing on a gobstopper listening to Mario Lanza singing "Golden Days." There was always a short film, the Pathe News, Pearl and Dean, trailers and the big picture.

Back then you were never going to the movies .It always going to the "PITCHERS."

And of course, whenever there was a cowboy film there used to be a thunder of stamping feet whenever the cavalry arrived to set the Indians packing and if someone was creeping behind the star of the film and our cowboy hero we would shout, "look out behind you."

I have memories of sitting there with a Lyons Maid in my hand watching the screen comedy antics of Ma and Pa Kettle or cowboy hero Randolph Scott, (pictured) who seemed to be in everything, beating every gunslinger under the saloon sun to the draw.

But the strange thing was I could pay my ninepence downstairs and one shilling and more upstairs and still walk in halfway through the big picture and walk out when it came around to that part again.

And I still enjoyed the plot.

I loved going to the "PITCHERS".

There wasn't a lot to do growing up in Nantymoel in the 1950s.

When I wasn't spending my wasted time hanging around the clock tower or watching Pricetown life go by sitting in the green shed there was always the "Mem" (Nantymoel Memorial Hall) and the Good Companions where I used to be a bit of a dab hand playing table tennis.

Back in the Nantymoel year of 1954 Doris Day was in the hit parade singing "Secret Love" and there was always the Top club or Band club outing to Porthcawl, Barry or Aberavon, where it always seemed to rain.

Every Sunday Mam would dress me up in my Sunday best and point me towards Horeb chapel.

Ahhh…. Horeb Chapel.

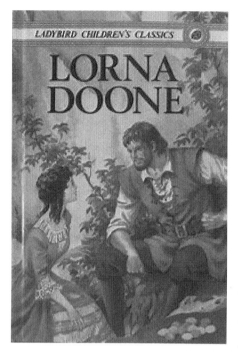

I will never forget one Christmas time at Horeb Chapel when Father Christmas paid a visit to hand out some presents. I couldn't wait to unwrap my present which was a book called Lorna Doone. I love, and still love the Lorna Doone book. John Ridd was my hero, and I hated the Doone clan.

And how can I ever forget the much-awaited Sheep Dip at "Danny the Farms".

It was one of the highlights of my young Nantymoel years.

Along with the club outing, Bonfire Night and the chapel Christmas party it was a Nantymoel event not to be missed.

I hardly slept a wink the night before.

I would get up wide eyed hoping that the weather would stay fine.

I would get there early not to miss the excitement reaching fever pitch.
To see the sheep being shepherded into the water was like a festival of fleece.

Just what was the Sheep Dip all about?
Well, I didn't know then, but I know now.
Sheep Dip is a liquid formulation of insecticide and fungicide which shepherds and farmers use to protect their sheep from infestation.
I can recall joining "The Band of Hope" when I was still wearing short trousers. The Band of Hope was founded in 1847 in Leeds to teach working-class children the evils of drink and promote abstinence. It also

organised outings, competitions and music for its members.

I'll also never forget the Park Street sporting days when myself Roy Ley and Rob Burgess would put more of a dap than a boot to a laced-up leather football.

We would spend hours slamming it against the wall at the back of the printer's shop.

And talking about my old schoolboy pal Roy Ley who has sadly passed away I can recall a time when he invited me into his house in Park Street to see something special.

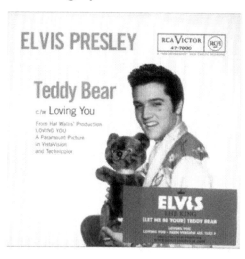

That "something" special was a radiogram.
I couldn't figure out what it was.
Anway Roy put a 78rpm record of Elvis Presley singing "Let Me Be Your Teddy Bear."

A radiogram by the music way a radiogram is a piece of furniture that combined a radio and a record player.

Radiograms reached their peak of popularity in the post-war era, supported by a rapidly growing interest in records.

And of course, on those Nantymoel rainy days you could always pass the time playing a Blow Football game.

Blow football I think was made by a company called Spears.

In many of my young days I used to be bent over the kitchen table blowing into a straw trying to put a ball into an opponent's net.

I never did get many net results.

Even better you could get friendly with a rich kid who had a Subbuteo table football set.

And there were days instead of being made to listen to "Mrs Dale's Diary" and "Much Binding in the Marsh" on the radio I got pally with a boy living a few streets away.

I soon discovered that his parents possessed this

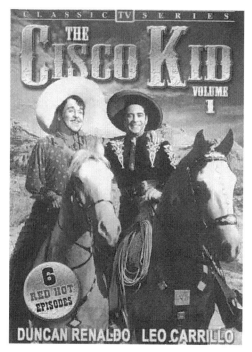 newfangled invention called a television set. And so it came to pass that whenever "The Cisco Kid", or sometimes "The Range Rider" was being shown on the telly he would invite me over.

"Ahhh Cisco....Ahhh Pancho."

They don't make them like that anymore.

And you know there were days when you really got lucky and got two packets of Wrigley's Juicy Fruit.

You got the packets when you got lucky and put money in the chewing gum machine when the arrow pointed forward.

I managed to stay pretty accident free in those young years except for the time I jumped off the Pricetown air raid shelter.

I was having a whale of a time until I landed on the grassy bank and my knees ended up under my chin and of course I happened to bite my tongue.

The result was my mother taking me to see Dr Schwartz where I had to have two stitches in my tongue which wasn't so bad really because I lived on ice cream for a few weeks.

In the year 1955 Cardiff had become the official capital of Wales and Dylan Thomas "A Child's Christmas in Wales" was posthumously published.

It was also the year that I had sat and failed the 11 plus school exam which caused my widowed mother a lot of heartache.

I would never get to wear the Grammar school tie and blazer my Mam was all ready to order at the Co-op while all her thoughts of her only son becoming a lawyer or a doctor and had well and truly gone out the front room window. Mam was inconsolable.

I remember our next-door neighbour, a lady called Martha, coming to see mam.

"Don't you worry Mary," she said putting an arm around Mam's shoulder.

"As long as he can count his change and get a job days regular, he will do alright."

Back in the 1950s when I was a regular reader of the Dandy and the Beano near the back of those comics was a page devoted to a company called Ellisdons. Ellisdons was a company that supplied jokes and tricks including such much wanted items as stink bombs, itching powder and a seebackroscope whatever that

was.

But the one trick that caught my good eye was called "How to throw your voice."

I had a bit of pocket money so I thought I would send off for it.

Every morning, I would anxiously for the postman, who would deliver before nine o'clock in those days, and finally the gadget arrived.

It was a small metal thing which you put under your tongue or whatever which would enable you to throw your voice.

I tried it umpteen times, almost choking myself on a few occasions, but my voice stayed put.

Eventually I did throw it-into the bin.

Back then I loved trying to assemble an Airfix model I might well have had for Christmas.

Mind you my Spitfire aeroplane or whatever never ended up like the picture on the box.

What sticks in my mind is that I used to end up with glue just about everywhere.

On the tips of my fingers and even worse sometimes on my mother's best tablecloth.

I always had trouble getting the cockpit in the right place.

And so, the next step in my schooldays venture was to walk through the gates at Nantymoel Secondary Modern, known more locally as the Park School, where I got my initiation by being hurled into "The Bush".

What a groundbreaking initiation that was.

Chapter 2
When Woodwork wasn't chicken feed.

SO the new phase in my schoolboy life was at the Park School.

There is one memory I have of the time I sat with the rest of the form in the Woodwork class under the supervision of teacher Mr Owen who I grew to have the greatest respect for.Mr Owen told the class to pick up pencil and paper and make a drawing of what we were planning to wooden carve out in class.

He had suggested items such as a magazine rack, a tea pot stand, an ash tray and so on.

As we were all sketching away, he walked around the class glancing at some of the drawings before stopping by one of them.

"What is that?" he asked a classmate.

"It's a chicken coop sir", he replied.

"Mmmm," said Mr Owen, "a chicken coop eh?"

"Yes sir."

"And where would we get the wood to build a chicken coop?" Mr Owen asked.

"You can order it sir,"

"Oh right. And how do you think we will be able to transport the chicken coop from the school to your home?"

"I know somebody who has got a van sir, and I know he would do it."

Mr Owen then whispered in the boy's ear:

"To be on the safe side just concentrate on making a magazine rack."

It could only have happened in the Park School.

While at the Park School I got friendly with a boy called Charlie Ham.

Anyway one morning in school assembly me and Charlie were fooling around when a booming voice from one of the teachers said:"Ham and Edwards go to the headmaster's room after assembly."

When he said Ham and Edwards, I thought for a minute he was going to say Ham and Eggs.

And so me and Charlie dutifully waited outside the headmaster's waiting for the inevitable. The inevitable being the cane.

The PE teacher back then was David Lewis and often he would have us playing touch rugby in the school hall which if I can remember correctly was more like "punch rugby".

A stranger turned up at one playing session who Mr Lewis introduced as a young teacher called Grahame Hodgson (pictured).

We were told that Grahame would be spending some time at the school.

Mr Hodgson was born in Ogmore Vale, and played club rugby for Aberavon RFC, Bridgend RFC, Exeter RFC, Exeter Saracens RFC, Teignmouth RFC, Torquay RFC and Neath RFC.

Graham Hodgson was capped 15 times for Wales between 1962 and 1967 while playing in the full back position.

Sadly, he died in January 2016 after a short illness, aged 79.

Every year the Nantymoel Secondary Modern, or to give it its more popular name the Park School, would hold a Sports Day on the Old Park.

To be honest I was pupil enemy number one to Mr Lewis the PT teacher.

I was useless at about every activity in the school gym.

I couldn't stand doing a handstand, was a flop at a flick flack and dreaded having to do a somersault over the wooden horse.

17

I used to beg my mother to write a note excusing me from PT but when I used to hand it to Mr Lewis he used to give me a stony, stare and say: "Collect your daps and get changed boy."

He was having none of it.

There were times when PT was the last lesson of the day me and another boy would hide in the toilets and escape by climbing over the railings into Gwendoline Street.

Anyway, back to the School Day Walking Event.

I could never win a zinc medal never mind a gold one because there was another boy who would always try and trip me up and I would do the same to him.

We were so busy trying to trip each other up that everyone would walk past us.

And then there was the Music class.

Try as I might I could not play a happy tune on a recorder

I did somehow get to play the opening bars of "Tom Hark".

"Tom Hark" by the musical way is an instrumental South African kwela song from the 1950s.

The song was arranged for the penny whistle, and I was later released in the United Kingdom after it was used as a theme on a television series.

It reached number 2 on the UK Singles Chart in 1958.

Another vivid memory I have is when I just happened to be on my own in the school cloakroom one morning when in walks this boy who looked every inch like The Fonz out of the TV programme "Happy Days".

He had it all.

The leather jacket, blue Jeans, white T shirt along with Brylcreem plastered hair tailed off with a DA.

"Give me your dinner money," he growled with his face just an inch or two from my NHS wired glasses.

"I..I..I don't have dinner money," I stammered," my mother is a widow so I get free dinners."

"Then let's have your fags," he snarled.

By now I was quaking in my daps.

"I swear I haven't got any. I smoked my last Anchor Tipped during play time."

Just when I thought he was going to pick me up and hoist me on to one of the cloak room hangers a teacher and a few pupils made an entrance.

"Everything alright there boys?", he asked.

"Yes sir," we both replied.

"Right then. Now why don't you pair get back to your classrooms".

I never went into the cloakroom alone after that.

After four years of trying to avoid PT lessons and managing now and again to smoke a Player's Anchor tipped fag in the school toilets, I was ready say goodbye to my school years.

I wasn't sorry to see them over.

Looking back what I enjoyed most were the English lessons.

CHAPTER 3

Apprenticeship.

IT was the summer of 1959 and I was 15 years old. The song "Smoke Gets in your Eyes" by the Platters was riding high in the charts while the film "Some Like It Hot" starring Marilyn Monroe, Jack Lemon and Tony

Curtis was being shown in the picture house in Nantymoel Workmen's Hall.

My Secondary school life had ended and so I found myself sat before a careers officer who needed to interview me.

"What job are you planning to do when you leave school?" he asked.

"A job as a newspaper reporter sir."

He gave a bit of a sigh and looked to the ceiling before saying: "Listen boy, you are never going to be a newspaper reporter.

"You simply won't have the qualifications.

"My advice is to go for a factory job down at Bridgend Trading Estate and if possible get yourself an apprenticeship".

An apprenticeship-that was the in working word back in 1959.

An apprenticeship by the working way back then gave school leavers a valuable opportunity to learn a profession through formal training

It was an opportunity to gain experience in the workplace and earn money at the same time.

As I walked out of the school gates for the last time, I made myself a promise that no matter what one day I would become a newspaper reporter.

I had finished school on a Friday afternoon and three days later on a miserable, misty, Monday at around 7am I found myself waiting in a Nantymoel bus station en route to Bridgend Trading Estate getting set for the first day of my working life.

While clutching my box of banana sandwiches and small bottle of Corona pop my thoughts turned to what lay ahead for me as a factory worker.

At the end of the half hour Western Welsh bus journey, I took my first steps inside a factory called Electrochrome.

My job on the factory line was to assist in dipping car parts and whatever into containers of chrome for the motor industry.

I never once whistled while I worked.I hated the job, the smell was getting right up my nose and I couldn't take my eyes off the very slow moving factory clock.

The time tortuously ticked by, and I just couldn't wait to get on the bus and back home.

I needed a job change and quickly and so after persistently protesting to my mother she finally gave in on the condition that I clocked out on that job and clocked in straight away on another.

I needed to get away from factory work and I didn't have to look too far to land a job with a glazing company in early 1960.

The job I was given is what was called a "shop boy" and my everyday task was shovelling up the glass off cuts which the glazers chucked under a bench while cutting glass to size. Occasionally I'd help a skilled craftsman who would cut the coloured pieces of glass that went into leaded lights used for special house windows and churches.

Leaded lights are decorative windows made of small sections of glass supported in lead frames.

One day all the glazers were out on jobs and the boss needed to go to a meeting.

Which left me on my own and in charge of an empty warehouse.

The boss told me that he was expecting a much-awaited urgent delivery of specially reinforced glass for a local jeweller's shop.

The boss hadn't been gone very long when a BRS (British Road Service) lorry pulled up outside loaded with the special delivery.

The glass, for the jeweller's shop, was in a wooden crate and the friendly driver told me that it was made by a company called Armourclad.

He said: "You can hit this glass with a sledgehammer, and it wouldn't smash but you have to be careful that you don't bang the corners, or it will shatter."

So, after I put my signature on his delivery note off, he went.

And so, I carried on shovelling and sweeping up glass but all the while looking at the crate containing the Armourclad,

Suddenly I took it into my head that I would get in the boss's good books if I unloaded the glass from the crate.

I tossed away my shovel and brush, gave my bucket a kick and decided to take the glass out of the crate.

I knew that I needed to be very careful so I put pieces of cardboard down to rest the corners of the glass on but somehow, I must have moved one of them with my size nine boots.

Carefully I got hold of the four-foot-wide glass and eased it out of the crate.

And then suddenly.... BOOM.

Instead of holding a four-foot-wide pane of glass I had my arms outstretched like an angler boasting about a big fish he had caught.

No more was there a pane of glass, instead there were thousands of pieces of glass on the shop floor.

For a while I just staggered around with my arms wide open still believing I was holding the glass.

I tried to hide before the boss came back but he did eventually find me and when he did, he gave me a lecture and it really was with both barrels.

Again, it was a case of job survival and somehow, I lived to shovel and sweep glass another day.

And then there was the wintry day that the glazers were putting windows into a technical college, and I was needed to light a fire to softly keep the putty from freezing.

While I was warming to the job one of the glazers, who was up a ladder, shouted that he needed more putty and quickly.

Without thinking I scooped up a lump of putty which wasn't warm but very hot.

The upshot was that I needed hospital treatment because the

piping hot putty had stuck to the palm of my hand which had become badly burnt.

But it wasn't all job doom and gloom.

I was called upon to assist a glazer, named Eugene, who was from the Ukraine.

It was a delight working with him.

Often, he would leap up onto a works bench and do a knees up in a Cossack dance.

He threatened to teach me how to do it, but it was always a dance step too far for me.

I kinda knew that I wasn't cut out to be a good glazer so after a few months I filled my last bin of broken glass and set my NHS glasses on another job.

And so along came 1961 when Merthyr born boxer Howard Winstone (pictured) won the World Featherweight title, Welsh born Rosemarie Frankland won the Miss World title and I was on the hunt for my third job.

One of my Vimto drinking pals was working at a factory in Bridgend Trading Estate called Walt and Engle.

He told me that there were jobs going there so I went for it and got one.

I really didn't fancy working in another factory.

But in the end my pal persuaded me to give it a try, so I went for it.

On arrival on my first day the foreman took me to a part of the factory where a machine was shooting out toy pop gun rifle barrels.

The foreman told me I just needed to stay by the machine, which cut lengths of pipe into one-foot-long barrels and shut it down if anything went wrong.

"Don't touch anything," were his final words before walking off.

Standing by the machine I thought back to my younger years when I was not only the proud owner of an Hopalong Cassidy watch but also a pop gun rifle which was attached with a cork on a piece of string which you would place into the end of the barrel.

When you fired the rifle, the cork would pop out of the barrel still on the end of the cord.

But when the toy memories faded the boredom kicked in.

And after the boredom came the curiousity.

There was a battery of different knobs and levers on the factory machine.

So, what did I do?

I just moved one of the levers.

It was then that all rifle barrel hell was let loose. Instead of the barrels being sliced in one-foot lengths they were now spewing out in three-foot lengths.

I tried put that lever back to where it was, but I must have turned the wrong lever because they were now down to six-inch barrels and to make matters worse, I forgot how the foreman told me to shut the machine off.

I was knee deep in rifle barrels before the frantic foreman came to my rescue and ended the barrel run.

I thought sure I would be "fired" after that, but I was given another chance when the foreman frog marched me over another part of the factory and another machine.

This machine was made up of a rotating tube covered in plastic.

My job was to get gloved up and hold some sort of wire which was wrapped around the plastic to make grooves in it which then become vacuum cleaner hose. I soon realised that if I stayed in this job, I would be driven clean out of my mind.

For years afterwards if I was anywhere there was a vacuum cleaner, I would give a long look at the hose and wonder if it was one of mine.

I thought job matters might improve when the foreman put me to work on a capstan machine.

Nothing to do with the Capstan cigarettes but a machine that created all sorts of fandangled things. I knew it wouldn't be long before I would capsize my capstan machine and get back on the job-hunting trail.

Growing up in Nantymoel the shopping language was never the "CO-OP" it was always the "COP".

My lovely mother was a regular customer at the Dinam Street "COP".

Mind you, if she couldn't manage to get to the "COP" my mother would send me down to the Bracchis (Henri Lusardi's shop) to get a quarter of lossins (sweets) among a list of other items.

In between the shopping times my mother would have friends call to the house while I would sit quietly reading my Tiger comic.

Some of the conversations between my mother and her friends will always stick in my mind.

Here are how some of them went....

Mam:"Duw I had a shock the other day".

Friend: "What's that then Mary?"

Mam: "Do you remember that man from up the valley who was sent to prison not long ago?"

Friend: "Yes."

Mam: "Well he's out in no time. I just saw him in the shop. Somebody told me he is out on patrol."

He was out on PAROLE-not patrol.

Here's another one.....

Mam: "You'll never guess what I was told today?"

Friend: "What Mary"?

Mam: "Do you remember that woman we were talking about the other day?"

Friend: "Yes I do".

Mam: "Well she's BURIED and she's dead."

For the life of me I think Mam got that the wrong way round.

And so, it came to pass when as per usual I happened to be supping a hot Vimto in a Bracchis with a pal when he said to me: "What are you doing working in a factory?".

"What's wrong with that?" asked me

"That's a woman's job that is. Why don't you get a job in the pit like me?".

"Mmmmm"

I was tempted but I knew my Mam would have none of it.

CHAPTER 4

"You are not going underground."

IT was 1962 when Z Cars was being shown on the telly, footballer Ivor Allchurch was named BBC Wales Sports Personality of the Year and Mam was not happy.

"You are not going underground so forget it."

"But Mam..."

"I don't want to hear one more word more about it."

Although two of my Nantymoel uncles had worked underground, Mam had always made it plain that I would not be working in the bowels of the earth.

But I didn't give up and Mam eventually relented, and I signed up for a job with the National Coal Board.

I had to undergo training for a few months at St John's Colliery in Maesteg.

I will always remember those days travelling from Nantymoel to Maesteg with Sam Cooke's rendition of the song "Chain Gang" very much in my head.

After finally finishing my training I found myself working on the surface of the Ocean Western Colliery in Nantymoel.

The Ocean colliery was only a short distance from my home in Cadwgan Street.

When the Wyndham colliery hooter sounded early in the morning, I would set foot on a path across a coal tip and head for the locker room on the pit head baths.

For many months I helped sort the slag from the coal in what they called the Screens.

In the Screens was a conveyor belt and my job was to pick out the slag from the coal before it was loaded into the railway wagons then disposed of on the colliery waste tips.

Sometimes the conveyor belt would stop, and things would go quiet. I recall that one stop time I felt kinda tired, so I sat down and started to cat nap.

While I was busy cat napping one boy working on the Screens decided to liven things up by having a bit of fun.

He suddenly jumped on to an open window and shouted: "That's it I've had enough. The Screens have done my head in."

Then he jumped out of the window.

There must have been at least a thirty-foot plus drop from the window to the ground.

We feared the worst

I rushed to the window fearing what might have happened to him.

When I looked out, he was sat on top of a wagon load of slag laughing his head off.

He must have jumped all of six feet.

During my colliery surface working days I also spent time stacking six-foot struts and spragging drams in the timber yard.

They were special working days working with special people including Len Bartle, Gordon Reed and Cliff Edwards

Len and I had become pals after working together in the timber yard on the surface of the Ocean Colliery.

We stacked every wooden item from "niners" to three-foot struts under the watchful eye of Gordon Reed
As it turned out we were more of an Odd Couple than Walter Matthau and Jack Lemon.

While I had just upgraded my wired framed NHS glasses and spent most of my non-working hours reading books and filling in crosswords, a leather jacketed, white Sloppy Joe'd Len was usually out riding his, I believe was a Triumph motorbike.

Len was a fully leather jacketed member of a motor bike gang who had decided to name themselves "The Ton Up Boys".

Anyway, it came to Pricetown pass that Len decided it was time for me to meet his "Ton Up Boys" pals.

Which as it turned out didn't go well at all.There was the small matter of me not having a motorbike.

To say I had some strange looks when Len introduced me was very much an understatement.

The boy who I thought must have been the Leader of the Pack said:"Listen, if you want to meet up with us you must do a ton (100 mph) on a motorbike.

"But I haven't got a motor bike," said me.

"Then you are going have to ride pillion on the back of a bike," said him.

I don't know who it was but one of them volunteered to take me on the back of his bike and get me my "ton up" pass.

And so, with shaking legs I got on the back of a Thunderbird or whatever motorbike it was and we headed for the Nantymoel hills.

Up we rode to the top of the Bwlch where the bike owner turned to me and said:"Okay once we get on the straight piece of road going towards Treorchy I am going to open her up and clock a ton."

I must have recited the Lord's Prayer a few times while thinking that the sheep on the side of the road would be the last thing I would ever see as the bike went faster and faster.

We couldn't be far from the Treorchy side of the Bwlch when he turned and told an ashen faced me.

"We did it we clocked over a ton."

Len, who has sadly passed away, and I became firm friends, and I have great memories of the times we spent together.

I never owned a motorbike although I did eventually buy a Lambretta scooter-but I never did get to do a "ton" on that.

I also have fond memories of working alongside Gordon Reed.

I remember one shift when Gordon arrived with a very close-cropped haircut.

I just happened to mention to him that I like his haircut and wouldn't mind having one like it.

He said: "I'm popping into Jack the Barbers after work so come along with me".

When we got to the barbers Gordon asked Jack to give me a haircut like his.

"Are you sure?"Jack asked me.

"Go ahead," I replied.

Anyway, I ended up looking being scalped and when I arrived home Mam wasn't happy with my new hair look.

If my 80-year-old memory serves me right, there were three men who regularly sharpened their scissors in barbers shops back then.

There was Sel Brown, Jack the Barber and one named I think Ornam Daniels.

And back in the 1950s to be a haircut above the rest you either asked for a DA, a Tony Curtis or a Crew Cut.

I used to have a Crew Cut and I did once ask for a Tony Curtis but when I got home and looked in the mirror, I didn't look anything like him.

But you know there is one haircut which I never had but what a lot of people used to talk about and that was the Basin Cut.

Ahhh yes the Basin Cut..I remember it well.

I mean to say a Basin Cut role model back then was silver screen legend Moe Howard, the boss of The Three Stooges.

Now Hollywood legend reckons Moe's haircut was

 achieved by accident. He was the youngest child in his family and his mother wanted a girl. When he was a child, his mother let his hair grow to shoulder length and she would delight in making it curly.

But Moe (pictured) could not put up with teasing he was getting at school, so he persuaded a friend to cut his hair by using a basin as a guide.

Moe liked his Basin Cut so used his head and kept it that way.

But it is a sign of the haircut times that the Basin Cut has taken on a posher version and is now known as the Bowl Cut.

And I think the Basin Cut, sorry the Bowl Cut, is making a haircut comeback because the haircuts some of the footballers are displaying today sure look like Basin Cuts to me.

The barbers used to be a place where you could sit down read a comic or two and listen in on who was getting the best veg out of their allotments.

They were good old Barber days.

All good surface things came to an end when I was told by a training officer that I would be going underground. The pit underground I mean.

I was teamed up with a gang working on a hard heading and although they were a great bunch I hated every minute of it.

It was shift work, days, afternoons and nights and I used to hate the afternoon shift the most.I vividly remember listening to Jimmy Rogers singing "In An English Country Garden" on the radio on a warm and sunny Nantymoel afternoon before trudging reluctantly along a tip pathway towards my pit head locker.

What I found strange about my short time underground was that myself along with many others were regular smokers but for the eight hours shift underground everyone coped without having a smoke.

But as soon as the shift ended there was a mad dash out of the cage to get to the canteen all "gasping for a fag and a cuppa".

I knew my mining days were numbered and so it was back to job hunting.

I think it was around the middle of 1962 at the age of sixteen that I managed to get a job with the Ogmore and Garw Urban District Council.

And what a job eye opener that turned out to be.

When I set my size nine boots in the Council yard in Ogmore Vale I was put to work on the ash cart before it became known as refuse collecting.

For the next couple of months in Evanstown, Gilfach Goch, which came under the Ogmore and Garw Urban District Council, I emptied ashes from buckled buckets into an open backed lorry.

I don't know how many times dust got in my eyes from a wayward wind and when not emptying ash buckets, I was tipping up galvanised rubbish bins.

So I was more than grateful when the council foreman more or less said I was rubbish working on the ash carts, and whispered in my ear that the sexton at

Ogmore Vale cemetery needed a hand digging graves. When I finally arrived at the cemetery gates and was led to where I could pick up my pick and shovel I was then taught how to dig a grave.

Oh Yeah! I needed to be trained to make the earth move.

When I was finally told to fill in my last grave I was given a middle of the road job painting white lines on the highways and byways of Nantymoel before spending a week or more weeding pavements.

I also spent some not so lazy,hazy days of Summer swinging a scythe while cutting back the grass on the banks of the road which led from Glynogwr to Blackmill.

I then realised I was going up in the council job world when I was drafted into the tarmac gang where I worked alongside Roy Evans and Dick Woosnam among others.

I never really got to lay any of the black stuff.

My job more often or not was to roast a shovel on an open fire so the tarmac wouldn't stick to it.

During my council working days I never knew from day to day what job I would be doing.

I suppose variety was the spice of job life.

Mind you I'll never forget when I popped home for lunch on August 5th 1962.

I had arrived back at my home in Cadwgan Street after a spot of pavement weeding when my mother told me that American actress Marilyn Monroe had been found dead in her Los Angeles home on August 4, 1962 at the age of 36.

I had fallen in love with Marilyn while sitting in the front row in the pictures in Nantymoel Workman's Hall.

I was so upset I didn't know what to think.

I was in such a state I couldn't even face finishing eating my egg and chips.

Another council job was helping a chap called Levi keep the Nantymoel side of the Bwlch mountain road free of falling rocks.

Levi was a bit of a Nantymoel legend, and I was looking forward to meeting him.

Levi had a little hut on the side of the road and every so often he would boot me out of his cabin to kick any fallen rocks off the road.

This needed to be done because it may prove a danger to motorists.

Back in those 1962 days there was nowhere near the amount of traffic travelling over the Bwlch as there is today.

But there were still occasions when passing motorists ended up with cracked windscreens from falling mountain rocks.

I also believe that back then there was always a dispute about whether insurance covered the damage or was it classed as an "Act of God.".

I enjoyed my Bwlch mountain time with Levi.

It was a great job by any road.

Mind you it was the winter of 1963 that made me think twice about seeing my working life out working for the council.

It was snowing heavily in the valley and the first highway casualty was the Bwlch mountain road.

A decision was made to make sure the road was made passable again and before I could finish my banana sandwich myself and a working pal were told to jump on the back of a chain tyred, flat backed, uncovered, lorry filled with grit and salt and head for the hills.

By the time we passed Levi's hut and got to the top of the Bwlch and began to descend the winding road the snowfall had turned into a blizzard.

We two were on the back of the snow blitzed lorry with shovels in freezing hands spreading grit and salt for all our worth.

When we eventually arrived back at the council yard my balaclava was frozen to my head, and I thought it would need a blow lamp to get me off the back of the lorry.

It was November 1963 and I was sat supping a hot Vimto with some pals in a Bracchis, which was in Ogwy Street.

I was trying to decide to take up the offer of being a bagged coal driver's mate.

Meanwhile café owner Mr Lusardi was listening to the radio. Suddenly he shouted across to us."Hey boys I just heard on the radio that President Kennedy has been shot while in a motorcade in Dallas." President Kennedy shot? I couldn't believe it.

We then bombarded Mr Lusardi with questions.

"Is he dead?"...."Who shot him?

I will always remember where I was when President Kennedy was assassinated.

CHAPTER 5
Memories of "Lynn the Leap".

WHEN I finally stopped hanging around the clock tower in Nantymoel and finished off my final Vimto at Lusardi's cafe my not so dancing feet headed toward the Palais de Danse in a busy Bridgend on Saturday nights.

If my failing memory serves me right the Palais was where you could have a jive in the downstairs hall or a Military Two Step on the upper level where I believe a chap named Henley Jenkins led the dancing way.

And then when Sam Cooke had finally finished
"Twisting the Night Away" you needed to be brave
enough to catch the last bus home from Bridgend.
And of course, if you failed to snatch a smooch at the
Palais there was always Saturday dancing nights at the
Grand Pavilion in Porthcawl.
The first drinking stop used to be the Jolly Sailor public
house before planting your battered blue suede shoes
on the Pavilion dance hall.
And when the sun sadly set over Sandy Bay and you
had missed the last bus home the next step was to find
somewhere to sleep.
There were few kipnapping chances.
The waste ground opposite the prom was usually home
to single and double decker buses and If you somehow
found one with open doors you were in with a chance
of slumbering on a seat.
The other method to put to rest your dozing dilemma
was to build a makeshift beach hut with deckchairs
which never really worked.
Those were the dancing days my friend I thought would
never end.

And so on to 1964 Richard Burton married Elizabeth Taylor (for the first time) in Montreal and BBC Wales Sports Personality of the Year was Nantymoel's very own Lynn Davies.

Lynn won an Olympic gold medal in the long jump in 1964 with a mark of 8.07 metres (26ft 6 in), earning himself the nickname "Lynn the Leap".

On the subject of Lynn there were Nantymoel Summer nights way back then when me and my gang would often walk past the Aber field which had a sand pit in it. And often when dusk was gathering, we would spot this figure doing long jumps into the sand pit.

"Davies is wasting his time again" is what we all thought.

How wrong were we.

And I suppose my only claim to nearly sports glory was being beaten on the baize by the boy who would go on to win an Olympic Gold Medal.

I reckon I was about 15 when I was smoking the last of my Woodbine while sitting in a billiard hall in the bowels of Nantymoel Workmen's Hall.

Suddenly this boy swaggered in and said:"Fancy a game of snooker butt?"

"Yeah why not," replied me.

I think I managed to pot a few reds and chalk my cue for the first time before he went potty and more or less cleared the table.

His name?

It was Lynn Davies, alias Lynn the Leap, alias an Olympic Long Jump Gold Medal winner.

It was also the year that I decided to take a job which gave me the sack on my first working day.

Although I had a good day's regular job with Ogmore and Garw District Council a pal I was working with persuaded me otherwise.

He told me that he had landed a job with the National Coal Board delivering bagged coal.

"I need a mate," said he to me,"why don't you pack the council job in and come with me."

So I did.

The first rainy morning on the job we arrived at the coal yard in Tondu where we were shown to a lorry and a pile of sacks.

We were given a delivery sheet and told to fill the sacks with coal.

And of course, to make matters more difficult we had to shovel coal off coal which was not easy.

Anyway, after we had filled and loaded, I don't know how many sacks off we went on our delivery rounds.

The first drop was at a school where I went in search of the caretaker to find out where the coal shed was.

"Go up those steps and go to the far end of the yard," he said, pointing yonder.

"Righto," I said.

"No wait.... I haven't finished," he said.

"At the end of the yard go up a few more steps which takes you to the far end of the top yard and the coal shed is there."

"What?"

And we needed to deliver 20 coal sacks.

Anyway, with coal sacks on our backs we went from steps to steps and yard to yard to reach the coal shed.

By the time I arrived at the coal shed I wasn't dropping the sack, I was collapsing with it.

I didn't care if I got the "sack", or they "fired" me.

My bagged coal delivery days were over.

CHAPTER 6
Over the Bwlch to "Las Vegas".

Pricetown Pals-Me and Mal and Roger Eggett.

In 1962 my mother, my Aunty Nellie, who was living with us, and me moved from Cadwgan Street and rented a house at the foot of Stormy Lane.

I remember it was a rather imposing, detached white house with a striking view and quite a big green frontage.The word on the Pricetown grapevine was that the house once belonged to a well to do Justice of the Peace.

Anyway, as we were settling in to our new home Mam noticed that a safe had been built into the living room wall.

"What do you reckon is in that safe?" asked Mam.

"Oh, forget it Mam," said me," whatever was in that safe is long gone."

But Mam was having none of it.She was determined to find out what treasures were in that safe.

One morning when she was shopping down Henri Lusardi's she happened to collar PC Dench and was able to persuade him to come and look at the safe.

When he came to the house, he took one look at the safe and said: "Believe me Mary that safe is empty. "Don't worry your head about it."

And so, we all lived happily in Stormy Lane for the next few years until....

The property's owner said we had to say goodbye to our "white house" because it was going to be demolished to make way for a garage to be sited there. Our next move was to a rented house in Waun Llwyd. Not long after we moved, the Stormy Lane white house was demolished and guess what?

The demolition people discovered valuables, including jewellery and important documents in the safe which was eventually "turned over to the state".

So Mam, who kept telling us "I told you so" was right after all.

The story about the safe's "treasure trove" did make a splash in the *South Wales Echo*.

The moral of the story..."Be safe and always believe your Mam."

Whenever I see a TV ad for a washing powder it always reminds of something which happened to me in the 1960s.

It is something which I have never "clean" forgotten about.

At that time there was there was an advert doing the rounds called The Daz White Knights.

Blokes calling themselves The Daz White Knights travelled around the country knocking on doors and offering £5 and £10 prizes to those housewives who had a packet of Daz washing powder handy.

Anyway, one afternoon my mother had popped out shopping and there I was alone in the house when there was a knock on the door.

When I opened the door there was this bloke standing there who said: "I'm a Daz White Knight-Have you got a packet of Daz washing powder?"

"My mother is not here so I don't know?" said me.

He gave me a look and a sigh before saying goodbye and off he went.

When my mother arrived home, I told her what happened-she wasn't a happy Mammy.

She marched me into the kitchen opened a cupboard and pointed at a packet of Daz washing powder.

So that was a fiver or maybe a tenner down the washing drain.

In 1963 myself, Gwyn Rogers along with brothers Mal and Roger Eggett decided to leave our worries near Nantymoel clock tower and direct our feet to find out what was "on the other side of the Bwlch Mountain".

I remember back then the Gerry and the Pacemakers song "You'll Never Walk Alone" was in the hit parade.

It could have been our theme song.

When we finished our five-mile walk and arrived in Treorchy on a Sunday night we thought it was Las Vegas compared to Nantymoel.

There were double-decker buses, wide roads and cafes open.

It was unbelievable.

There was even a place called "The Coffin" where they held dances on a Sunday night.

Paradise found.

For the next three years, when we couldn't thumb a lift, come rain, snow or shine, we would tramp the tarmac from Nantymoel to Treorchy.

I suppose we were indeed the "Pricetown Pilgrims" who somehow discovered a whole "new world" back in the 1960s.

Instead of spending our teenage years swigging Vimtos in a Nantymoel Bracchis and kicking our heels around the clock tower.

We decided to find out what form of life lay on the other

side of the Bwlch Mountain.

And that is when a lifelong adventure began.

And so, it came to Bwlch pass that if we couldn't get a lift, we would walk the six miles from Nantymoel to Treorchy three or four times a week.

The downside was that after enjoying the Rhondda nightlife there was a sinking feeling about having to walk the six miles back home.

One late Sunday night I arrived at Dom's cafe in Treorchy for the usual meet-up to find that "there they were gone."

No sign of Gwyn, Mal or Roger.They must have got a lift.

So it meant that I would be going solo over the Bwlch which I was not at all walking looking forward to.

I remember it was a moonless night with the mist slung low over the top of the Bwlch.

I had just about reached the misty mountain top when I heard footsteps coming from behind me.

The mist was so thick I couldn't see the Rhondda lights behind me nor the welcoming Nantymoel lights in front of me.

Suddenly the footsteps got nearer and louder.

Oh my God!

Could it be the beast of the Bwlch or perhaps a Yeti on the loose.

I thought my Nantymoel number had come up

I was just about to break into a run when this rather big figure emerged from the mist and with a booming voice shouted.."Hang on Dai boy. Wait for me."

It was Ray Vaughan.

At the time Ray was also a regular visitor to the Rhondda.

It was with the sheerest of reliefs I walked with Ray the rest of the way home.

Ray was as big as he was gentle.

I was saddened to hear that he had passed away.

The last time I saw Ray was when I was travelling through Treorchy.I very much wish I had taken the driving time out to have a chat with him.

I always enjoyed Ray's company, particularly on that misty Sunday night many years ago.

Chapter 7

A uniformed job.

IN 1965 my growing up in Nantymoel years ended when I married a Rhondda girl and settled down to start a family in Pentre.

I soon found a job with a company who were installing the heating at a Rhondda school.

The job was great while the company's contract lasted which wasn't too long.

And so, one morning after being given the heating heave ho I called into the Labour Exchange in Pontypridd to see what was on offer.

While there I was told that the Pontypridd and Rhondda Joint Water Board were on the lookout for labourers.

For a couple of months, I dug ditches for plumbers and jointers to repair pipes until a vacancy came up in the depot for a job as a Turncock in the Rhondda Fach.

A Turncock by the water way is defined "as a waterworks official responsible for turning on water at the mains while repairs are being carried out".

It was a uniformed job, and I suppose I looked a bit like inspector Blakey from TV's "On the Buses" while flushing hydrants and turning mains water on and off.

MR WATER THE TURNCOCK.

Then there was the time that a leaking underground water pipe needed repairing so when the jointer and his gang finally unearthed the problem pipe the water needed to be turned off.

And so it was my duty to warn householders in several streets that the water was being shut off.

Having done that I shut off the valves so the pipe was dry, and the repair could get done.

All the time I was keeping a close good eye on my watch because I needed to catch a not very often bus to my home in Pentre.

With minutes to spare I was given the thumbs up to say the repair was done so I raced around to turn the water valves back on and just managed to hop on my bus.

Later at home while watch watching "Coronation Street" there was a sharp knock on the door.

It was my supervisor, and he wasn't happy.

He told me that his phone had been jammed with calls from people saying their household water supply had been off for a couple of hours with no sign of it coming back on.

"But I turned the water back on" I protested.

"You didn't turn it all back on," snapped him,

"You only opened two valves instead of three leaving a couple of streets without a water supply."

Part of my duties was to knock door after door warning people that their water supply was being shut off whenever work was being done to repair a main water pipe.

And guess what I discovered?

When you tell many householders that the water supply is being shut off for two hours what do they do to find out when the water supply will come back on?

They turn a cold water tap on and wait for the water to gush through.

And so it came to pass that a water main needed repairing in a very posh part of the valley.

As was my duty I knocked every brass knocker on some very nice houses to use my poshest voice to give my "water going off" warning.

But then this happened.

A lady living in one of the houses decided to pop out and do some shopping while the water supply was off. Before she went out, she did the usual thing and left a cold water tap open in an upstairs toilet but unfortunately, she left the plug still in the sink.

And while she was out what did I do?

I turned the water back on.

By the time she arrived back home the sink water had brought down a lot of her lounge roof as well as causing other damage.

She tried to sue the Board for a shedful of shekels, but her case was never "watertight."

My Job with the Water Board turned out to be a "pipe dream" and so I managed to land a job on a building site in Cardiff.

The job was with contractors who were building a warehouse.

And so, on my first day there me and another bloke were put to work digging a trench.

It wasn't a case of whistle while you work but I thought it would pass the paying time if I had a chat now and again with my fellow digger.

But he didn't want to know he just gave me a cold sort of stare now and again.

Thankfully the end of the shift didn't come soon enough, and I was glad to hang my pick and shovel up. It was then that a police van pulled on to the site and two officers jumped out and escorted my digging pal into the back of the van.

"What's happening there?" I asked one of the workers.

"Oh..he's a prisoner."

"Prisoner? What do you mean prisoner?"

"He's doing time in jail, but he is given a day release to work on the site as part of some sort of rehabilitation programme."

"What's he inside for?" asked me.

"Manslaughter," said him.

"MANSLAUGHTER?" gulped me.

From then on, I only spoke when I was spoken to by him and I always made sure to offer him some of my banana sandwiches.

Very soon it was on to the next job.

I somehow managed to land what I thought would be a premium job with the Refuge Insurance branch in Treorchy.

I think I must have been the only insurance man doing his rounds on a two stroke Lambretta scooter.

I soon realised that my insurance job was not going to be for life and in 1971 I managed to find employment as a paint sprayer in the T.C Jones factory in Treorchy.

Of course, 1971 was the year of the power cuts which meant that for a period I was doing extra-long shifts at the factory

I was put to work with a chap called Idwal who was a dab hand at spraying red oxide paint on steel girders. As for me? I was useless at it.

My girders had more runs than the Glamorgan Cricket team.

I remember working the night shift when the works targets were reached sometimes around four in the morning it usually signalled for many to deal out the cards for Three Card Brag.

The factory may have long gone but the memories haven't.

And do you know I almost became a Rhondda bus conductor?

I spotted a vacancy for the job, and I was invited to an induction day at the Rhondda Transport office in Porth.

It proved to be a "single" journey for me because after the induction day I never returned.

I was amazed at some of the things I heard at the meeting.

For instance, the trip most feared by drivers and conductors was the last bus journey up to Gilfach Goch on a Saturday night.

I don't know why that was!

I also don't know why I didn't take the job.

I suppose because it didn't "ring any bells for me"

Chapter 8

When I wasn't top of the pops.

IT would have been sacrilege if my boyhood Sunday dinners in Nantymoel were laid without a glorious glass of Corona pop.

Nantymoel pop nectar then included Dandelion and Burdock and American Cream Soda.

Which reminds me...

Back in the 1970s I was a "picker" in the Budgens Food warehouse in Talbot Green.

My job as a warehouse picker was to travel up and down the food warehouse while filling containers with food, detergents and goodness knows what, which would be loaded on to a lorry before being transported to shops.

I may have been a picker by day but every Monday evening I earned some shekels doing a two-hour shift in the "Thomas and Evans" warehouse in Porth.

My job there involved loading crates of Corona pop on to a lorry ready for delivery next day.

After I finished my shift at Budgens I would fire up my Fiat car and head for Porth.

It was only a Monday evening job, but the extra cash was handy.

Anyway, one night I somehow slipped while carrying a crate of pop and the next minute I was flat out on the floor.

After hearing the crash, bang and bit of a wallop the manager came rushing out of his office and shouted: "What's happened?"

My work pal who was stacking the crates on the lorry shouted back: "Been a bit of an accident boss. Dave has just fallen while carrying a crate of pop."

To which the boss shouted back: "Are all the bottles safe. There had better not be any broken."
Always knew I'd come off second best against Corona pop.

It must have been in the very early 1980s when I somehow managed to get a Saturday afternoon job as a field steward when the Wales rugby team were playing in Cardiff.

My memory seems to think that it was called the National Stadium then and not Cardiff Arms Park.

When those far off Saturdays came, I had to be at the stadium at noon where myself along with the other stewards were given the lowdown by the chief steward on where we would be placed inside the ground and what we would be doing.

And what a "trying" time that could sometimes be.

My usual stewarding spot was keeping my good eye on the crowd behind the goalposts.

During the hour before kick-off everyone was in a rugby happy mood with plenty of singing, sometimes a band playing and even a cockerel crowing when the French were the visitors.

But nearing the start of the match some sozzled spectators would kick off.

You could spot them a drop kick off.

They were always very drunk with some wearing pit boots with a miner's helmet on carrying a big leek and with one goal in mind to get on the pitch.

Despite warnings to "stay put" they would clamber over the barrier and start running around the field chased by stewards.

But not me-I kept my head under the North Stand parapet.

I mean to say it was no laughing matter with BBC cameras zooming in on the ground previewing the match.

Who wanted to be seen as a stupid steward seen hopelessly hot footing after a lunatic legging it over the halfway line?

One afternoon us stewards got together and came up with a crafty plan to tackle the rugby runaways.

There was one who we knew was the pitch invading ringleader.

He would always start the running game off, and others would follow.

So, a couple of the super fit stewards volunteered to stop him in his tracks and make an example of him. About 30 minutes before kick-off, he bounced over the barrier and was on the pitch.

He hadn't reached the 25-yard line before the stewards tackled him and handed him over to the chief steward who would make sure he didn't do a repeat performance by escorting out of the ground.

"That's him done for," thought me.

Wrong!!!

It was all quiet on the rugby front until 10 minutes later when unbelievably the very same ringleader had got back into the ground got his leg over and was triumphantly running around the pitch again.

At the end of my stewarding shift I was paid £3.

In 1981 found myself being a back door security man in the Co-op store in Pontypridd.

And what an experience that was!

My job was to check the proper furniture, fancy goods, electrical, food and what have you being delivered to the back door was all in order.

One day the store detective was away attending a meeting, so the store security responsibility was handed over to me.

Come the afternoon I got a call that the drapery department manager needed a word.

He pointed out two women who he said had put some items in a bag and hadn't paid for them.

And so it came to pass that I did my Inspector Clouseau bit and followed the two women on tip toes from department to department to see if there was any sign of them handing over cash.

They didn't.

When they eventually stepped outside the store I pounced.

"Scuse me," I said," Can I have a word?"

"What's the problem?" asked one.

"I've reason to believe you have taken clothing items from the store without paying for them.

" What are you on about?" said angry one.

"Do you mind opening your bag?" asked me.

"HERE", she snarled, shoving her open bag almost up my left nostril.

It was fully empty.

I couldn't believe there was nothing in it.

"I'm sorry there's been some sort of mistake," I stammered.

"There's been a mistake all right and that mistake is you, "she screamed.

"Our husbands will be waiting here to sort you out when you finish work."

I went back to see the drapery manager who told me "He could have sworn that they had put items in the bag."

Oh Yeah!

I should have finished work at 5pm that day but I decided to hang around until the stars came out. My days as a security officer were well and truly numbered.

Chapter 9
A newspaper reporter at last.

IN 1983 Swansea born singer Bonnie Taylor had a smash hit with the song "Total Eclipse of the Heart" and Keith Deller became World Darts Champion. As for me!

I fulfilled a boyhood dream and became a newspaper reporter.

It was while I was on a banana sandwich break while working in a Co-operative store in Pontypridd that I discovered the *Rhondda Leader* newspaper was on the lookout for district correspondents.

I was living in Trealaw in the Rhondda at the time so I thought I would give it a writing go and after submitting a few columns Jim Campbell the editor asked if I would pop in and have a chat with him.

He told me that he needed someone to write a rugby column for the *Pontypridd Observer* and asked if I would like to do it.

I didn't hesitate in taking up the offer and so every week I would write a column for the *Pontypridd Observer* under the headline..."Scrum Down with Ted Edwards".

I was given the name Ted because I was not a fully qualified journalist so I could not use my proper name.

I always wanted to be a "Teddy Boy" so there you go.

Every week I would make telephone calls to local rugby club secretaries to gather all the latest gossip for my column.

After a few rugby column writing months had gone by Jim Campbell, came up with another offer.

He said:" I wouldn't mind taking you on as a reporter, but you would need to full time attend South Glamorgan Institute of Higher Education in Cardiff and get a post grad degree in Journalism for that to happen".

So, I found myself at the South Glamorgan Institute.

A 38-year-old sat among teenage wannabe newspaper reporters.

A lecturer then entered the room and introduced himself.

He then began questioning everybody about their past education.

One by one the young trainees spoke about the universities they attended and then it came to my turn.

The lecturer asked: "And what about you David. Where did you attend?"

"Nantymoel Secondary Modern", I answered.

He quickly moved on to the next trainee.

For two long months I had to burn the midnight oil to keep pace with the young trainee reporters.

By some miracle I managed to pass my Shorthand test my Law test a Feature Writing test and a Local Government test.

So that was it I had finally become a newspaper reporter.

The following five years I reported on news and sport for the *Pontypridd Observer* and the *Rhondda leader* newspapers before a change of reporting direction took me to the north of England

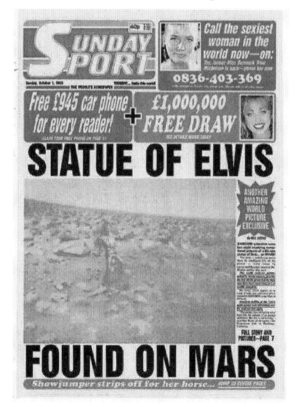

While there I worked for a free newspaper called the Blackburn Citizen and also did a Saturday shift for the Sunday Sport newspaper.

After two years I put my final full stop to a Citizen

story and motored back to Wales to take up a reporting post with the newly launched *Swansea Gazette* newspaper.

After finishing my reporting stint in West Wales, it was a change of direction for me because I joined the staff at a Bridgend based Press Agency.

After spending a year there, I was on the reporting road again this time covering stories for the LWT Press Agency based in Whitchurch near Cardiff.

From there I took a reporting job I couldn't refuse with the Cardiff based Hills Welsh Press Agency.

Although I was kept busy with Press Agencies, I wasn't getting the same job satisfaction I was while working for newspapers.

With my Press Agency days behind me I joined the reporting staff with an Aberdare based newspaper called *News of the Valleys*.

The job didn't last long however when the newspaper permanently folded.

It wasn't long before I was scribing away again with a free newspaper called the *Caerphilly Chronicle.*

Yet again the pagination life of this newspaper was very short, and I soon became aware that I needed to

nail down another job.

And then….

I got a phone call offering me a reporting job with the *Rhondda Leader* newspaper.

I had come full reporting circle.

And it was at a desk in the *Rhondda Leader* newspaper office in Pontypridd that I ended my reporting days when I retired in 2012.

Looking back, I have had a wonderful reporting life. Someone somewhere once said "If you love your job, you will never do a day's work."

Which is very true in my case.

Chapter 10
Precious memories of Fay.

I HAD my fair share of being on the other end of complaints during my years reporting for the *Rhondda Leader* but as is often said..."You can't please everyone".

But among all those complaints would come along a word of thanks which then made the job worthwhile.

But there was one big thank you which came my way in 1994 which was more than special.

Fay, my daughter from my second marriage, was not at all well and eventually she underwent hospital tests to find out what the problem was.

It was initially thought that Fay had aplastic anemia but further tests proved that she had leukaemia.

For several weeks I regularly needed to take Fay to the Heath hospital in Cardiff for blood transfusions while she awaited a bone marrow transplant.

It meant dividing my working hours with hospital visits while my daughter was having treatment.

Some weeks had gone by when I had a phone call to say that the managing director and the editor in chief of Celtic Press were coming to the Ponty office to speak to me.

"Oh...Oh..there may be trouble ahead," I thought.

I couldn't have been more wrong.

They were there to tell me that in appreciation of the work that I had put in, despite the stress I was under, they were offering me an all-expenses paid holiday to take Fay anywhere in the world she wanted to go when she had got better.

Fay was in hospital waiting for a bone marrow transplant when I gave her the news.

Her face lit up and she chose Disney Land in Florida.

Fay did eventually get a bone marrow transplant from someone on the Anthony Nolan register.

The bone marrow transplant failed and in January 1995 my angel of a daughter died at the age of 18.

During my reporting life I did many distressing stories on people who had lost loved ones and now it was something that I had to deal with.

I will always cherish the memories of Fay, and I will always be hugely grateful for the brilliant gesture I received from the company I worked for.

Acknowledgements.

One person I would like to offer my sincere thanks to is Russell Farmer who gave me this brilliant painting of Nantymoel he did to use on the front cover of my book.

Printed in Great Britain
by Amazon